NoLex 11/12

Florence Griffith-Joyner

by Mark Stewart

PHOTO CREDITS

All photos courtesy AP/Wide World Photos, Inc. except the following:

Focus On Sports – Cover, 4 top left, 4 bottom right, 6, 24, 27, 29 top, 30, 33 left
Tony Duffy/Allsport – 23 top left, 33 right, 41 bottom left, 46
Allsport – 23 bottom, 41 top right
Mike Powell/Allsport – 5 bottom right, 26
Mitchell B. Reibel/Fotosport – 25
Lori Adamski Peek/Fotosport – 9
Florence Griffith Joyner Youth Foundation – 43
Mark Stewart – 48

STAFF

Project Coordinator: John Sammis, Cronopio Publishing
Series Design: The Sloan Group
Design and Electronic Page Makeup: Jaffe Enterprises, and
    Digital Communications Services, Inc.

LIBRARY OF CONGRESS CATALOGING-IN-PUBLICATION DATA

Stewart, Mark.
    Florence Griffith-Joyner / by Mark Stewart.
        p. cm. – (Grolier All-Pro Biographies)
    Includes index.
    Summary: A biography of the United States Olympic track and field star known as "FloJo."
    ISBN 0-516-20227-8 (lib. binding)–ISBN 0-516-26047-2 (pbk.)
    1. Griffith Joyner, Florence Delorez, 1960-   –Juvenile literature. 2. Runners (Sports)–
United States–Biography–Juvenile literature. 3. Sprinting–Juvenile literature. 4. Olympics–
Juvenile literature. [1. Griffith Joyner, Florence Delorez, 1960-   2. Runners (Sports)
3. Afro-Americans–Biography. 4. Women–Biography. 5. Olympics.] I. Title. II. Series.
GV1061.15.G75S84   1996
796.42'092–dc20
[B]
                                                                          96-28190
                                                                             CIP
                                                                              AC

Grolier **ALL-PRO** *Biographies*™

Florence Griffith-Joyner

by
Mark Stewart

CHILDREN'S PRESS®
A Division of Grolier Publishing
New York • London • Hong Kong • Sydney
Danbury, Connecticut

Contents

Meet Florence Griffith-Joyner

She has been described as everything from intelligent, artistic to ambitious and aloof. She has been hailed as the fastest woman in the world. She has even been credited with revolutionizing her sport. Her fans, however, just call her "FloJo." Her name is Florence Griffith-Joyner, and this is her story . . . "

Growing Up

When Florence Griffith looks back upon her childhood, she remembers a house full of love and a neighborhood full of tension. She was the seventh child born to the Griffiths, who lived in the Watts section of Los Angeles, California. Watts was a poor but proud community comprised mostly of African-American families. During the 1960s, its residents protested against racial prejudice, and they often clashed with police. Florence remembers how passionate her older brothers were about these issues. Florence's passion, however, was running.

Riots in the 1960s destroyed much of Watts, where Florence grew up.

All her life, Florence has run faster than other people.

Florence first discovered the sport when she was seven years old. She began competing in races sponsored by the Sugar Ray Robinson Youth Foundation. Robinson, a former boxer, was one of the greatest African-American athletes in history. He believed strongly in giving kids a chance to build self-esteem through sports. Florence loved how it felt when she was out in front of the other runners, with the wind whooshing past her ears and through her hair. From then on, she ran almost every day, and soon she could beat almost anyone, including most of her older brothers!

Florence's parents were divorced when she was young. Even though her father spent a lot of time with his children, Florence became especially close to her mother. They would spend hours together sewing dresses for Florence's dolls, and she would tell her mother about her dreams. "We really couldn't afford new Barbie clothes, so my mother taught me how to sew and how to make my own dresses," Florence says. "That was such a joyful time for me—doing something creative that we both loved."

Florence and her three sisters wanted her father to move back home. "Sometimes we would pretend that Barbie and Ken were mom and dad," she remembers. "We'd put the dolls back together hoping that our parents would get back together, too." But that never happened.

Florence's mother was an independent woman who set a strong example for her daughters. "After she separated from my father, my mother had no choice but to be independent, and I think I got that from her—being able to stand on my own two feet," recalls Florence. "She taught us all that nothing is going to be handed to you. You have to make things happen."

Florence loved playing with dolls as a child. As an adult, she had her own line of dolls.

Jesse Owens was one of the greatest U. S. Olympic heroes.

oon after enrolling at Jordan High School, Florence joined her older sister, Elizabeth, on the track team. When Florence was 14, she entered the Jesse Owens National Youth Games, which were named after one of America's greatest Olympic heroes. She won the sprint competition, beating many older runners. A year later, she won the competition again. At Jordan High, she broke most of the school's sprint and long-jump marks. By the time Florence was 18, her times in the 100-yard and 220-yard dashes had approached world-class status. But being a great athlete was just one of many things that Florence wanted to do. She dreamed of becoming a clothing designer, or maybe a psychologist, and she loved to paint and write poems. One day, she hoped to own her own greeting-card company. Florence knew that she could only gain the knowledge and expertise to pursue her dreams by continuing her education in college, so she enrolled at California State University in Northridge, just north of Los Angeles.

College

Bob Kersee helps his wife, Jackie Joyner, before a race. Bob was Florence's coach at UCLA, and Jackie was a close friend.

One of the first people Florence Griffith met at Cal State-Northridge was the university's track coach, Bob Kersee. He was aware of her talent in track and field, and he urged her to develop it. Florence was not happy in college and dropped out during her freshman year, but Coach Kersee talked her into coming back. Sadly, she injured herself that spring and had to miss the entire 1979 season. But by then Florence had become committed to her track career. She worked hard to improve for the 1980 Olympic Trials, hoping to win a spot on the team that was supposed to travel to Moscow. She just missed

Years

making it, finishing fourth in the 200 meters. As it turned out, the U.S. team never competed in the 1980 Olympics. President Jimmy Carter declared a boycott against the Soviet Union and did not allow American athletes to compete in the games.

When Coach Kersee accepted a job at UCLA, a school with one of the nation's top track programs, Florence followed him there. Very quickly her life began to change. Among the many new friends she made was Jackie Joyner. Florence already knew Jackie's brother, Al, whom she had met at the 1980 Olympic Trials. Al Joyner, a master of the difficult triple-jump, was very happy that Florence had decided to attend UCLA. He thought she was the most incredible woman he had ever met. He was not very happy, however, when Florence began dating fellow track star Greg Foster. He was heartbroken when Florence and Greg announced their engagement.

Florence was fast becoming one of the country's top female athletes. In 1982, she was a member of America's record-setting World Cup relay team, and she took individual honors in the 200 meters at the NCAA Championships. In 1983, she won an NCAA title in the 400 meters. She also won several 100-meter sprints during this period. These three races demand different skills and techniques, yet Florence was terrific at all of them. After graduating from college with a psychology degree in 1983, she joined Coach Kersee's World Class Track Team and began preparing for the 1984 Olympics.

Florence had taken huge steps toward two of her childhood dreams. She was one of the fastest runners in the world, and she had completed the initial training required to become a psychologist. Next, she would tackle clothing design. She began making her own racing outfits, and they were quite unlike anything anyone in the sport had ever

Florence edges Nebraska's Merlene Ottey to win the 1983 NCAA 400-meter championship.

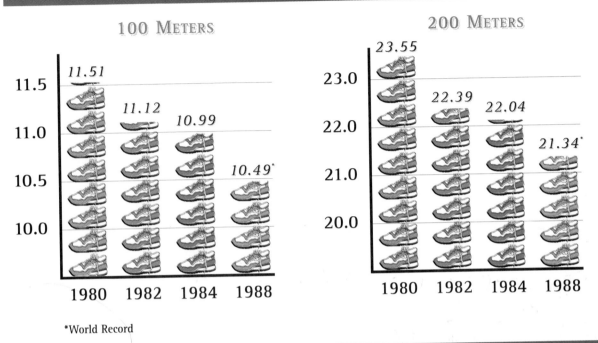

100 METERS

1980	1982	1984	1988
11.51	11.12	10.99	10.49*

200 METERS

1980	1982	1984	1988
23.55	22.39	22.04	21.34*

*World Record

seen before. They featured explosive colors, interesting fabrics, and imaginative cuts. In every event Florence entered, all eyes were on her as she approached the starting line, mingling with other runners, who wore traditional shorts and tank tops. Florence also liked to paint her super-long fingernails to complement the colors of her outfits.

Florence was part of a star-studded track team at UCLA, including Evelyn Ashford, who won gold at the Olympics.

The Story

Florence Griffith made the 1984 U.S. Olympic team in the 200 meters and won a silver medal that summer in Los Angeles. She was disappointed that she did not win the gold, especially in front of all the friends and family who had come to watch her compete. Although she came away from the Olympics with just one medal, Florence had become an international sensation.

Florence waits for the start of the 200 meters in the 1984 Olympics, where she took a silver medal.

Continues

Over the next two years, Florence continued to race. In order to support herself, she took a full-time job at a bank, and also did part-time work as a manicurist and hairdresser. By 1986, she was training less and less, and soon she was 15 pounds overweight. Then her engagement to Greg Foster ended. Although Florence still competed in track events, she was starting to lose interest in the sport.

Al Joyner changed that. After winning the gold medal in the 1984 Olympics, he had returned to his home state of Arkansas. In 1986, he moved to Los Angeles, where he renewed his friendship with Florence. The more they hung around together, the more they realized how much they had in common. They began dating and soon fell in love. In October 1987, they were married. Florence took Al's name and kept her own, too, becoming Florence Griffith-Joyner. That was a mouthful for most track fans, so they simply started calling her "FloJo."

Al and Coach Kersee pushed Florence to get back into peak condition. At the 1987 World Championships, she made headlines by winning two medals in her hooded bodysuit, yet Al believed that she was only scratching the surface of her potential. By the fall of 1987, Florence was ready to commit herself totally to becoming the fastest woman in the world. With the help of Al and Coach Kersee, she began a grueling training program designed to have her in peak form.

Florence recalls, "I had always come in second, and when you've been second best for so long you can either accept it or try to become the best. I made the decision to try and be the best in 1988."

At the 1987 World Championships, Florence competed in a hooded suit.

Florence arrived at the Olympic Trials with a good chance of making the 200-meter team. What she accomplished over two blistering hot days in July was incredible. Competing in the 100 meters, she crossed the finish line of her first race in 10.60 seconds—the fastest time ever recorded! But when officials found that she had been running with a 7-mile-per-hour wind at her back, the record was eliminated. In her next race, however, Florence broke the tape at 10.49 seconds. When officials checked the wind monitor, they could hardly believe their eyes: it read 0:00, which meant that Florence was officially the fastest woman in history. No one has ever come close to breaking this mark.

"I had a good start, a relaxed middle, and kept my knees up at the end," she says. "It was more or less a perfect race. When I saw that time, I couldn't believe it, but after the first race time I knew I could get into the 10.50's. It just made me realize that if I kept concentrating, I could go faster." The next day, Florence made the U.S. team in

Coach Kersee hugs Florence after she established a new world record for the 100 meters during the 1988 Olympic Trials.

the 100 meters and 200 meters. In each of her 100-meter heats, she had beaten the world record that existed at the start of the trials. In the 200, she broke the U.S. record with a time of 21.77 seconds.

Florence continued her dominance during the Olympics in Seoul, South Korea. In the 100 meters, she set a new Olympic record in her very first heat. When she streaked across the finish line in the final to win the gold medal, she had a huge grin on her face. Some say she even let up a little at the end. In the 200 meters, Florence broke the Olympic record in the semifinals, then put up another record time in the final. She had entered two events and won two gold medals with ease. Then Florence won her third gold as a member of the winning 100-meter relay team. She had achieved every goal she and Al had set for her before the Olympics, but she was not done yet.

Florence received news that one of the runners on the U.S. 400-meter relay team had pulled a hamstring muscle and could not compete. The final was to begin just an hour after Florence had won the 100-meter relay. Could she step in? No problem, she said.

Florence sets a 100-meter Olympic record at Seoul.

Florence beat out nine outstanding amateur athletes to win the 1989 Sullivan Award.

Barton Biondi Blair Boitano Evans

Jones Griffith-Joyner Kiraly McClain Smith

Florence took the baton for the final leg of the race and tried to make up the two-meter difference between herself and the leader. Florence ran as fast as she could, but could finish no higher than second. With the silver medal, Florence had an incredible four medals to her credit.

In April 1989, Florence announced her retirement from competitive athletics. Nine days later, she was given the Sullivan Award as the nation's finest amateur athlete. Over the next few years, she pursued many of her dreams outside of sports. Florence started her own clothing company, released a line of cosmetics, and wrote more than two dozen children's books. She also tried her hand at acting, appearing on hit television shows such as "227." "Now that track and field is moving down on my list," Florence explains, "the other things are moving up."

What lies ahead for Florence? Wonderful opportunities to explore and grow continue to come her way. Her boundless talent and appetite for adventure guarantee that she will make the most of those opportunities.

Timeline

1984: Wins Olympic silver medal

1987: Marries triple jump champion Al Joyner

1983: Graduates from UCLA

1988: Wins three golds and one silver medal at Seoul Olympics

1996: Is enshrined at MGM studios at Disney World

1989: Receives Sullivan Award as top U.S. amateur athlete

Florence's performance in 1988 made her a national track hero.

Track

Florence's 1988 gold medal in the 100 meters surprised everyone, even though she recorded the fastest American times in the event in 1985 and 1986. "I was never allowed to concentrate on the 100. I was always somewhat overlooked."

Growing up in a poor neighborhood, Florence realized that she would only go as far as her legs, her mind, and her heart would take her. "Nothing is going to be handed to you—you have to make things happen."

Action!

Florence is all business on the track.

According to Florence, she and Al are the perfect couple. "We have the same views about track-and-field and about life."

Although Florence is gracious and friendly during competitions, she prefers not to chitchat with other runners. "I don't play around. I want to get on the track, get the job done, and get off."

Florence's winning smile in the 100 meters captured the hearts of a worldwide audience during the 1988 Olympics. "That smile came from within, because at that point, about ten yards from the finish line, I knew that I had the race won."

F lorence measures her athletic success not by victories, but by the pride and enjoyment the sport has given her. "I've been in track and field for more than 20 years, and out of all my races, I've lost more than I've won. But it's been fun."

Florence's leg strength allows her to burst out of the starting blocks.

F lorence credits a grueling weight-training program for the vast improvement in her starts during the 1988 season. "In order to burst out of the blocks, you need a lot of leg strength."

27

Dealing

When Florence Griffith-Joyner set her world record during the 1988 Olympics, many people wondered how a 28-year-old was able to blow away younger runners. Although Florence passed all of the tests for banned substances, rumors spread that she had enhanced her performance through the use of steroids. Forced to defend herself, she chose not to lash back at her critics. Instead, Florence delivered an inspiring message to young athletes everywhere.

"I was very hurt. It bothered me. I am anti-drug, I do not use drugs, and I don't think a person has to use drugs. I trained a lot harder—maybe three times harder—for the '88 Olympics. There is no substitute for hard work . . . I have the medals to prove it!"

Florence easily wins a 200-meter heat at the 1988 Olympics.

With It

Florence credits her strength to hard training.

HOW DOES

Toward the end of a race, Florence seems relaxed while others struggle.

She Do It?

Florence Griffith-Joyner went from being a good runner to being a great one thanks to an amazing discovery she made prior to the 1988 Olympics. By studying champions such as Carl Lewis, she noticed that you could actually gain more speed by not straining so hard.

"For a long time I thought that being relaxed meant you were running slow, but it's the contrary. When you're trying to go fast, you're fighting against your body instead of letting go. Relaxation was the key."

American track star Carl Lewis

Designing

Other runners may surpass Florence Griffith-Joyner's brilliant record, but none will ever cut such a stunning figure in the starting blocks. The running suits she created revolutionized the sports apparel industry, and made her one of the world's most well-known designers. Florence's most striking outfit was a low-cut body suit that left one leg completely exposed.

"I like designing clothes, and I wanted to bring something of myself into what I do. The one-legger? That was an accident. I was actually creating an even more radical style by cutting several holes in the stocking, and I happened to cut off the leg. I tried it on and thought, 'Hmmm, this looks cute.'"

Woman

Family

Al Joyner and Florence are all smiles at the 1988 Olympics.

Florence Griffith-Joyner is a member of track's most successful family. Her husband, Al, became the first American in 80 years to win an Olympic gold medal in the triple jump. His sister—and Florence's dearest friend—Jackie Joyner-Kersee, is regarded as one of the finest all-around track athletes in history. Jackie is married to Bob Kersee, who was Florence's former coach!

Matters

Although Florence's parents divorced when she was a child, both were strong influences on her life. From her mother she learned to be independent and take responsibility for her own life. From her father, she learned the importance of discipline and got her drive to constantly improve. Florence feels that, by taking an interest in their children's athletics, mothers and fathers can become closer to their kids. "Parents need to be role models for children and instill in them the fact that exercise and healthy eating should be lifelong habits."

President George Bush greets Florence and her daughter, Mary.

Say What?

Here's what track people are saying about Florence:

"She's so sincere and sweet, but she's the most determined athlete I know besides my sister, Jackie."

— *Al Joyner, Florence's husband*

"It's a great feeling as a coach to see your athlete run well, hearing the oohs and aahs as she picks people off."

— *Bob Kersee,*
Florence's former track coach

"For a long time, we've been thought of as 'jocks.' Florence brings in the glamour. She walks out on the track like she owns it."

— *Wilma Rudolph,*
1960 Olympic gold medalist

"The gods were with her. . . . It was an unbelievable time."

— *Carl Lewis,*
who witnessed FloJo's
record 100-meter run

"Florence's 10.49 and 21.34—those records will never fall."

— *Gwen Torrence,*
Olympic gold medalist

Career

Florence (second from right) and teammates celebrate their 400-meter relay win in the 1987 World Track and Field championships.

F lorence Griffith-Joyner has set sprinting records that could last a long, long time. More important, she helped to create business opportunities that had never existed before. Her enormous worldwide appeal proved that people will listen to what African-American female athletes have to say, and consumers will buy the products they endorse.

Highlights

In 1981, Florence won a silver medal in the 200 meters at the U.S. Nationals. She won the silver again in 1982.

Florence won the silver medal at the 1984 Olympics in Los Angeles, California.

Florence streaks to a 200-meter world record during the 1988 Olympic semifinals.

Evelyn Ashford (left) takes a hand-off from Florence before running to victory in the 4 x 100 relay at the 1988 Olympics.

Florence's first major victory came at the 1987 World Championships, when she was a member of the gold-medal U.S. relay team.

Florence won three gold medals at the 1988 Olympics in Seoul, South Korea. She also won a silver medal filling in for an injured runner in the 4x400 relay. Her 21.34 time in the 200 meters established a new world record.

lorence was named 1988's Female Athlete of the Year by the Associated Press and *Track and Field News*. She also won the 1989 Sullivan Award as the top amateur athlete in the United States.

FloJo takes a victory lap in Seoul.

Florence's medal collection at Seoul included three golds and a silver.

Reaching

Florence Griffith-Joyner understands the importance of setting goals and knows how hard you must work to attain them. For many years, she and Al spoke to kids at schools and youth organizations, and many of those kids went on to do wonderful things. But somehow, this was not enough. They dreamed of doing even more. In the fall of 1992, this dream became a reality when the Florence Griffith-Joyner Youth Foundation was established.

Florence says, "We help young people set goals, and then provide them with the emotional, educational, and financial support necessary to attain those goals. We teach kids to be proud of themselves, and show them ways to relate to others so they can have fun while they develop positive self images. The message we try to get across? Your dreams deserve a try . . . the sky's the limit!"

The programs offered by the Florence Griffith-Joyner Youth Foundation are designed to help young people get the

Out

most out of each day, while working toward the ultimate goal of making a positive difference in society. These programs include music and singing, arts and crafts, creative and performing arts, a math and science club, and the foundation's own track team. Florence is especially proud of the "Fight to Be Fit" program, which helps young people establish healthy lifestyle habits.

Florence says, "We reinforce what they are learning in the classroom, while exposing them to opportunities they may not be getting in school. For instance, we can provide kids with paid work experience, or enroll them in our Mentor Program. And each year, ten kids who distinguish themselves both in school and the community are awarded scholarships. We view it as a wise investment. After all, the youth of today are the citizens of tomorrow."

Numbers

Name: Florence Delorez Griffith-Joyner

Nickname: "FloJo"

Colleges: University of California at Los Angeles
California State University at Northridge

Height: 5' 10"

Weight: 150 pounds

Born: December 21, 1959

Florence's career peaked at just the right time, as she grabbed international headlines at the 1988 Olympics. Here is a look at how she fared in some of the major events she entered over the years:

Year	Competition	Event	Finish	Time
1981	U.S. Nationals	200 meters	2	23.09
1982	U.S. Nationals	100 meters	3	11.15
		200 meters	2	22.58
1983	U.S. Nationals	200 meters	3	23.23
	World Championships	200 meters	4	22.46
1984	U.S. Nationals	400 meters	3	51.56
	Olympics	200 meters	2	22.04
1987	U.S. Nationals	200 meters	2	21.70
	World Championships	200 meters	2	21.96
		4x100 meter relay	1	41.58*
1988	Olympics	100 meters	1	10.54
		200 meters	1	21.34**
		4x100 meter relay	1	41.98*
		4x400 meter relay	2	3:15.51*

*Team time/** World Record

Glossary

APPAREL clothing

BANNED SUBSTANCES illegal drugs

BOYCOTT to join together and refuse to deal with a person, business, or nation

CLASH to come into conflict with; to fight

CONTRARY opposite; reverse

DOMINANCE reign; position of power

HAMSTRING MUSCLE any of three muscles at the back of the thigh that are used to flex and rotate the leg and to extend the thigh

NCAA National Collegiate Athletic Association; the governing body for college sports

RADICAL unusual; extreme; not traditional

STATUS positioning; rank

STEROIDS drugs containing hormones—although they aid in building up the body quickly, they are outlawed for use by most athletes because of their deadly side-effects

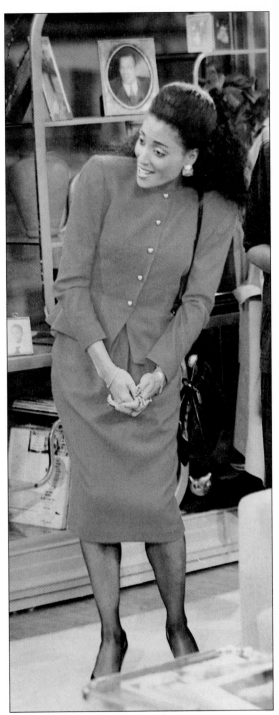

Index

About The Author

Mark Stewart grew up in New York City in the 1960s and 1970s— when the Mets, Jets, and Knicks all had championship teams. As a child, Mark read everything about sports he could lay his hands on. Today, he is one of the busiest sportswriters around. Since 1990, he has written close to 500 sports stories for kids, including profiles on more than 200 athletes, past and present. A graduate of Duke University, Mark served as senior editor of *Racquet*, a national tennis magazine, and was managing editor of *Super News*, a sporting goods industry newspaper. He is the author of every Grolier All-Pro Biography.